THE SPIRIT
IS
THE COSMIC ALL - POWER

MALCOLM L. LANDRY

DEDICATED

TO

"THE GODDESS"
YVONNE ELAINE LANDRY

AND

"THE IMP"
MARC HILL

Foreword

Magic and self-discovery are imbedded here. These epic, rhythmic words will encode themselves deep in your soul and will lead you to great understandings when you least expect them.

Here is a gentle roadmap. We find the beginning, as always, is right where we are. You can't just follow – you may have to lead. And where you go with it can have depth and breadth and expansion and consciousness shifting of mythic proportions.

Those who learn from the signs along this enlightening path will win the brilliant treasure, and it will be gold for your life.

Discovery will first come as a whisper from your soul, next it will speak with your own voice from your heart, finally when you had almost forgotten the question, the answer will explode into your life.

This is a brilliant discovery piece. You will want to read it again and again.

W. Robynne McWayne, M.D
Willow Springs Ranch, Nevada
Author of "Radical Reality"

THE SPIRIT
IS
THE COSMIC ALL - POWER

BY

Malcolm L. Landry

Trafford rev. 10/22/2021

www.trafford.com

North America & international
toll-free: 844-688-6899 (USA & Canada)
fax: 812 355 4082

PROLOGUE

By in large we who inhabit this world are not actively aware, consciously, of our connection with the one who made it. It is like we are walking around here actually not knowing how we got here, why we were brought here or what we are doing here. Most of us believe that the people who are called our parents are the ones responsible for it all; but the people who are called parents are in the same identical kind of ignorance as are the ones that are called their children. It is almost as though we do not know who we really are because we do not really know who is responsible for our being here. It is hoped that this state of affairs can be altered.

Spirit Is The Cosmic All - Power has been purposefully written to complement, interpret, simplify, illuminate and most of all validate our most intimate experiences (particularly the intuitive ones) that we are having (and cannot talk about for various reasons) at every one of our living moments. It is true that our divine parent, the divine parent of our spirit, is always and continually related and/or directly connected with us so intimately as to be no different as the connection that a baby has with its mother when that baby is in the mother womb. This relationship is immutable (unchangeable) and it is real (immutable reality). We are currently (and have ever been) in direct communication with this reality as it has been informing us every since we have been alive. We are probably unaware, asleep to, or possibly afraid of the inner and intuitive experiences that we are having continuously with this reality of the immutable Spirit that we are.

Upon the realization that the Human Spirit is Human Life and is divine; we will realize that we do not need to earn the right to live; and these words shall be understood to no longer be a statement of economic heresy but a statement of liberation and truth. Once the people of this world understand this fact, survival will crumble and an unending abundance will flourish in its place. Spirit Is The Cosmic All – Power is a story in poetry. It is the human story of a lost and forgotten spiritual legacy and heritage written exclusively in a first of its kind, metered rhyme. This book has been rendered in a poetic verse structure designed specifically to appeal to two basic attitudes of human reason: Insight and Justice. It is a poetic rendition that topically and subjectively delves into our current orientation to life. It elaborates upon the realities of apprehending life correctly and also pursues to reorient us out of the disorientation that has been our past and presently our confused state or way of living. Poetically this book is designed to generate in the reader a revelation by delivering insight about the reality of our identity as the Spirit and our connectedness to the cosmic all. A restitution of the spiritual legacy and heritage is initiated by a clarification of the injustices currently in practice and suggestion by clarification of the means to access justice by being free of the injustices. The idea is to stimulate readers with the inspiration to be who we have forgotten ourselves to be.

Since the pursuit of this project (or mission) of "The Spirit Is The Cosmic All - Power", I have been predisposed to delivering this "revelation of Spirit" as a threefold message. The poetic purpose here is to deliver a message about the universal Spirit, namely we are it. The poetic principal (reason) behind this book is to deliver a message about spiritual objectives, namely our Soul is "for" ever. The poetic plan is for readers to re-member and to re-understand a message about a new beginning for "the becoming" because "The Bodies Are Here". "The Spirit Is The Cosmic All - Power", "The Soul Is 'For' Ever" and "The Bodies Are Here" lists some of the titles that are associated with the next nine books in which it is hoped that a complete delivery shall be accomplished with the message for which I have undertaken to be responsible.

For the last four years it has been my continual endeavor to undertake the creation of a method, style, tone, etc for the delivery of this message. Two years ago, as the research and effort began to formally gel into patterns of poetry, the information was entitled "The Spirit-Soul-Body" and was copy written online until September 2003, when the dilemma that was experienced at that time force a discontinuation of online activity and a more in-depth approach was researched and discovered by the first week of November, 2003. At that time it was realized that all of the material could not be effectively contained in one volume entitled "The Spirit-Soul-Body". Other considerations lead to the realization that an entirely different entitlement, method, style, tone, pattern and delivery was needed. Then, after a Thanksgiving dinner, upon being introduced to a book written by W. Robynne McWayne entitled "Radical Reality", a profound realization of the connectedness of the material with us all caused a shift of perspective. It was from this experience that the trilogy of which "The Spirit Is The Cosmic All - Power" as the first publication became a vision. The material that came forth, from the first week of December 2003 until the body of the first book was completed, came into being almost like what has been called automatic writing. To me it appeared as though I was totally aware as the writer that I was the one composing and writing the material while the material was being written. However, all who had contact with me during the thirty-three days that it took me to complete it commented repeatedly upon how obsessed and possessed I appeared to be; and, by hindsight, I have had to admit that I have, upon no other occasion in my life, written any of the material that I have written as prolifically as I did during this time. The objective that I was most aware of during my effort to get this material into words was the message and it delivery for which I hold myself responsible.

How we end up categorizing this book is less important than how we end up using it. It is my suggestion that we use it as a tool to awaken ourselves and not as a new kind of lullaby to continue to nap by.

By Malcolm L Landry
Author/Writer/Poet

THE TABLE OF CONTENTS

CHANGE YOUR **PERSPECTIVE** ON LIFE
AND
ALL OF YOUR **PERCEPTIONS** OF LIFE WILL CHANGE
WHEN
NOTHING CHANGES – NOTHING CHANGES

INTRODUCTION

1: SPIRIT

SPIRIT IS – >

THE COSMIC ALL

IS SPIRIT

The Spirit is the cosmic all
And also a divinity
In power love and what is called
An intelligent trinity
"I AM" and "I WILL" and "I DO"
The trinity around the true
Containing electricity
Magnetism and gravity
In dualities that relate
Realities that radiate
But force-energy vibrations
Together forms a relation
With the one – a union station
Of being in situations
Experienced with elation –
But no one is supposed to know
About the Spirit or grow
With the knowledge of the flow
Of actions that achieve the goals
Of the Spirit by inborn souls

INTRODUCTION

1: SPIRIT

SPIRIT IS

THE COSMIC ALL – >

IS SPIRIT

The Spirit is the cosmic all
And when re-creation begins
The living divinity called
The universe begins within
Then appears the mind and the soul
With bodies inside filling goals
Mind and soul within the Spirit
And bodies within endear it.
Beautiful bodies that flatter
Us all with a lovely matter
But you probably didn't know
About divine Spirits or grow
Up learning early how to show
Spirit daily and come and go
Conscious of the Spirit in flow
That's probably why the entire
Spiritual goal to aspire
To now remains so undesired
Remains as yet to be retold
Remains unknown yet to unfold

INTRODUCTION

1: SPIRIT

SPIRIT IS

THE COSMIC ALL

IS SPIRIT – >

The Spirit is the cosmic all
And Soul is forever "to be"
And bodies are here to recall
Objectives for eternity
Powerful throbs and vibrations
Pulsation and undulations
Indicate lively vigor, vim
Influence, strength and might that stems
From joint and combined blends
Of the oneness that life intends
But marriage amalgamations
Harmony in corporation
Coalition situations
Concurrent expectations
Agreement manifestations
As taught is false intelligence
Knowing no wise of common sense
Nor understands the performance
Behavior exploits or the needs
Conducting feats of Soul in deed

INTRODUCTION

2: DIVINITY

THE SPIRIT – >

THE QUALITY

ELECTRIC

Divinity is the Spirit
The sacred as the life of light
All love and holiness is it
All as all of cosmic delight
Divine is power and above
All intelligence with all love
The quality of trinity
In Spirit is divinity
In the Spirit of sacred facts
Rest the Spirit of the acts
But all are here taught to believe
That only the gods may conceive
Divinely – all have been deceived
Into believing all will leave
With death and might only receive
Life with birth but no entity
Will partake of the trinity
Of life as a divinity
Though each being alive will find
It's self as Spirit and divine

INTRODUCTION

2: DIVINITY

THE SPIRIT

THE QUALITY – >

ELECTRIC

Divinity is quality
Living the life of the ever
Living as a trinity
With a forever endeavor
Being timelessly infinite
A basis for the sentient
Divinity is the life giving
Life as alive to the living
And when life-lovers endear it
They know divine as the spirit
But what is here being revealed
Has mostly always been concealed
So all would not believe the real
So all would not desire or feel
Divine as the Spirit or wield
Power love or intelligence
Neither even some common sense
Nor the divine rights that were meant
For all as of the royalty
For all as a divinity

INTRODUCTION

2: DIVINITY

THE SPIRIT

THE QUALITY

ELECTRIC – >

Electric is divinity
Exciting all-ness with the best
Magnetic as an entity
A cosmic all attractiveness
As universal gravity
Grounding life for living to be
Electromagnetic powers
Alive to be "I AM" towers
Primarily - as the gravity
Remains unknown in faculty
But if everyone could know
Of powers and forces that flow
Through divinity or that grow
With each being from birth below
The threshold of things – all would go
Directly to the divine source
Of living life or they would voice
And obtain by a divine choice
Exactly what fancifully
They would select decidedly

3: ELECTRICITY

CONSIDER – >

THE EXCITING

LIVING ALIVE SELECTION

INTRODUCTION

Consider electricity's
Aspect in the universe
Phenomenal sentiency
Of power that many rank first
Of the energy trinity
Life-force vibrations "to be"
Electric qualities translate
Divine Spirit into the states
And rates of vibrated force
Through which the energies can course
But no one will explain or tell
Or otherwise inform or spell
Out how electricity dwells
Here as such or truly excels
To impel expel or repel
According to all wills or ways
To speed things up or to delay
Eventualities that may
As an objectivity be
The use for electricity

INTRODUCTION

3: ELECTRICITY

CONSIDER

THE EXCITING – >

LIVING ALIVE SELECTION

Electric is the exciting
It is of the reality
Of life living the inviting
Thrill ... shocking the meaning to be
Electric is the active choice
Behaving as the spirit's voice
Flowing current as most recent
Basis of every event
Spectral from which the rays of light
Frightfully startle with delight
But electric was not divine
Not supposed to be behind
Cosmic motivation or find
Universal systems to bind
Or else otherwise be assigned
The most primary of life roles
As motive divinity goals
By which the Spirit can unfold
The universe and all the things
Cosmic electricity brings

INTRODUCTION

3: ELECTRICITY

CONSIDER

THE EXCITING

LIVING ALIVE SELECTION – >

An "alive" living selection
Expression of a soul's desire
An act of choice and election
Electricity is fire
Divine in Spirit as the pick
Of force and powers called magic
Electricity as the mark
Of true Spirit is the spark
Of life – it is in truth a sign
In life of the truly divine
But we're not taught of electric
Life – we are told it is magic
Or an unexplainable trick
Phenomenal - an emphatic
Unknowable - even tragic
If it is morally abused
Or maybe socially misused
But maybe all can be excused
If all left electricity
To those who teach untruthfully

INTRODUCTION

4: MAGNETISM

FORCEFULLY – >

SPIRIT TRINITY

THE POWER OF LOVE

Magnetism is forcefully
A cosmos of attractiveness
As Spirit and divinity
Mysterious receptiveness
Inside the universe as draw
Throughout the cosmos without flaw
It is the force of all appeal
The charming energy concealed
In vibrations that "en-trance"
And captivatingly enchant
But all of us know all too well
How secretly is kept the spell
Enigmatically it dwells
Hidden from all. No one will tell
Why magnetism can compel
Action so mysteriously
And all so inscrutably
Yet like all other energies
Magnetic likes will be repelled
And unlikes join by force compelled

INTRODUCTION

4: MAGNETISM

FORCEFULLY

SPIRIT TRINITY – >

THE POWER OF LOVE

Part of the Spirit trinity
Magnetism has been defined
As basis for activity
A foundation for the sublime
Glamorously charismatic
Compellingly enigmatic
Enticingly Unknowable
Alluringly unshowable
A spiritual possession
Of the power of selection
But all are not taught how to use
Inner magnetism to choose
As all of us have been refused
The knowledge – so – now all will lose
Out and will also be confuse
About – how – part of trinity
This basis of activity
This Magnetic reality
Of magnetic power giving
Divine life – gives to the living

INTRODUCTION

4: MAGNETISM

FORCEFULLY

SPIRIT TRINITY

THE POWER OF LOVE – >

The love power is magnetic
An attraction known but unseen
A drawing so enigmatic
It defies science and it seems
Though almost diabolical
Completely undeniable
It is a total persuasion
Gripping every occasion
Do imagine how the flowers
Develop magnetic powers
But there's talk about birds and bees
The glamour sensed around the trees
The charming that can be received
With power - but none can believe
For all have been truly deceived
About magnetism's power
And how "about" all it towers
Like a charismatic flower
Over all within the Spirit
Making all within endear it

INTRODUCTION

5: GRAVITY

SIGNIFICANCE – >

WITHIN

EXPRESSES

Significance is Gravity
Seriousness and magnitude
Third aspect of the trinity
Divinity with attitude
Duration with implication
Within Spirit gravitation
A prime part of the cosmic all
The reason why things seem to fall
The Spirit of solemnity
Exist as cosmic gravity
But none may correctly relate
The facts about gravity's state
And no mystery is as great
Or so enormous in its weight
As gravity – today the fate
Of truth rest with those who would lie
About the powers and defy
The law of truth – they would imply
That the import of gravity
Means only gross severity

INTRODUCTION

5: GRAVITY

SIGNIFICANCE

WITHIN – >

EXPRESSES

The center of all is within
Each one – the cosmic universe
Of Spirit combines all and blends
All using gravity at first
To connect the divinity
By completing the trinity
Gravity is a magnitude
Within enormous solitude
It is the quality of weight
That unerringly gravitates –
But it is a magnanimous
Place of being in all of us
That we have yet been taught to trust
By those who know but ever lust
After power – also the thrust
Of those upon which all relied
Having been entitled "The Wise"
Concealed reality with lies
Concerning the validity
Living within called gravity

INTRODUCTION

5: GRAVITY

SIGNIFICANCE

WITHIN

EXPRESSES – >

Spirit expresses gravity
It is the within without weight
Ultimately sincerity
Inside meaning within fate
It is interiority
Inside divine reality
The basis of value and worth
Consequential meaning of birth
Within implication command
With gravity to understand
But these thoughts are misdirected
And this knowledge is protected
Kept secret - none may inspect it
Now all are taught to reject it
So that no one will connect it
With divine truth functionally
And use the meaning worthily
Because the force of gravity
When used with common sense
Will bind love with intelligence

SECTION I

6: POWER

FOREMOST – >

DIVINITY IS

TO BE

Definitely first and foremost
Spirit is the cosmic power
It is the universal host
And over the all it towers
Divine – the "I AM" trinity
Lives as power cosmically
Vibrations energy and force
Make up the power by which choice
May not in this life be divorced
From the divinity of force
But we are not personally
Supposed to understand or see
How to be spiritually
As sufficient powerfully
As those who know how secretly
To "in the spirit" manifest
Spirit as power – how to best
Use the power of consciousness
To come to spiritually
Understand all endearingly

SECTION I

6: POWER

FOREMOST

DIVINITY IS — >

TO BE

The power is divinity
The divinity of "is-ness"
The Spirit of the life – "to be"
The power used in consciousness
Power motivationally
Powerful significantly
Power electromagnetic
Powerfully energetic
And this is why none can resist
The "I AM therefore I exist"
But power is the first and last
Of subjects that have been bypassed
Of knowledge taken out of class
Of the inner learning that has
Not been allowed to be amassed
As one would the information
Given as public relation
To restore the situation
When the Spirit ceased to flower
Within all as conscious power

SECTION I

6: POWER

FOREMOST

DIVINITY IS

TO BE – >

The power "to be" is Spirit
And is spirituality
"The life" and no one should fear it
Being "the choice" powerfully
Though power looks like arrogance
When it appears with confidence
Know the intimacy was meant
Because power is so intent
As the Spirit is inherent
So is power divine content
But don't you see - if you were told
About power and could unfold
Spiritually divine roles
To fulfill the pre-chosen goals
Of your Spirit's powerful soul
Those who lied about power could
No longer deceive and would
Leave all to be - because they should
Not block the power of Spirit
Nor teach the "know-not" to fear it

SECTION I

7: I AM

IDENTITY

THE ALL-COSMIC SPIRIT

TRINITY – >

"I AM" the part of trinity
With the "I WILL" and the "I DO"
Of personal divinity
Fulfilling the sacredly true
The divinity is surely
Personal in you and is purely
The power that none may resist
The "I AM" therefore I exist
The personal reality
Powerfully "I AM" to be
But the social authorities
Do not allow all to perceive
Of being all – they would deceive
And not permit all to believe
Nor do they want all to conceive
"I AM" all of reality
Electromagnetically
"I AM" the real powerfully
"I AM" the all when the motive
Displays that all is relative

SECTION I

7: I AM

TRINITY

IDENTITY – >

THE ALL-COSMIC SPIRIT

"I AM" the first identity
Here to Spiritually be
The universal entity
Of this cosmic reality
This person here with character
This entity that we refer
To as me myself and as I
When we speak of Spirit and my
Ego or my I-D or sometimes
This aspect of my divine mind
But "I AM" really not supposed
To know my self or to impose
True knowledge because if I chose
To – deceivers would be exposed
Authorities would be deposed
And leaders would lose the control
Over life and their social roles
As truth concealers would unfold
As Spirit wakes up to deduce
It's self to be power and truth

SECTION I

7: I AM

TRINITY

IDENTITY

THE ALL-COSMIC SPIRIT — >

"I AM" the all-cosmic Spirit
Or how can I be another
Nor should none within me fear it
Being I and father-mother
Living moving being the call
Of cosmic Spirit – I am all
"I AM" first in the trinity
Of being and doing willingly
"I AM" both a mother spirit
And the father of all of it
But "I AM" known by you to be
A within-ness that you call me
You feel interiority
Understood so intimately
As "I AM" that you might not see
Yet that you contain the within
Within you and have never been
Content "inside-ness" or as in
You are - though not taught about it
Non-content container-Spirit

SECTION I

8: ELECTROMAGNETISM

UNIFIED DUALITY – >

ABOUT PRISMS

ELECTROMAGNETICALLY

A unified duality
Of personal power Spirit
Electromagnetically
Gives life and powers all with it
Most common are energies from
Force vibrations of this spectrum
This electromagnetic ray
Functions primarily today
As the mainstream for energies
And the force vibrations in deed
But those who maintain ignorance
Do so because they take the chance
To make you pay as they enchant
You with the lies that they advance
Maintaining within you the trance
That you cannot possess the sense
To apprehend the evidence
Without help - that your conscience
Lacks the real and the power
Spectrum as the Spirit's flower

SECTION I

8: ELECTROMAGNETISM

UNIFIED DUALITY

ABOUT PRISMS – >

ELECTROMAGNETICALLY

Some only know about prisms
Or how white light is refracted
Yet electromagnetism
Embodies light and is active
With six other forcing powers
Within this spectrum that flowers
Vibrating a duality
Electromagnetically
A multiplicity of waves
Of being in a spectral phase
But this was not supposed to be
Seen or viewed spiritually
Living in fact powerfully
Was reserved politically
Not for consumption publicly
Unless and until people pay
To access the power today
Pay they must in every way
And be confused about Spirit
So that they may ever fear it

SECTION I

8: ELECTROMAGNETISM

UNIFIED DUALITY

ABOUT PRISMS

ELECTROMAGNETICALLY – >

48

Electromagnetically
Spectral and a duality
Power's motivationally
Primary in a trinity
Of power spectrums consisting
Within Spirit and emitting
Two more divine groups of dual
Spectrums that provide the fuel
Living within divinity
Sacredly as activity
But electromagnetism
Soon becomes capitalism
Because the selectivism
Of western socialism
Teaches not relativism
Because here only money talk
And those lacking the motive walk
Aimless as the power poor stalk
Politics and the religions
Seeking a motive provision

SECTION I – PART I

9: VIBRATION

SPIRIT POWER – >

RAYS OF ALL

ULTRAVIOLET

The Spirit's power vibration
As divinity manifest
Pulse and throbbing undulation
Not withstanding all of the rest
Have the triune and sacred signs
Of Spirit vibrations divine
Vibrations that are spectral
In a universe textural
Within a cosmos of Spirit
Know that power will vibrate it
But we are not told when seeking
Vibrations that we are meeting
Spiritually and greeting
Power in the Spirit speaking
Powerfully and completing
The manifested universe
But what is unknown and adverse
About this truth is that the worse
Kind of lying authorities
Are lying to keep all in need

SECTION I – PART I

9: VIBRATION

SPIRIT POWER

RAYS OF ALL – >

ULTRAVIOLET

Rays of all manifestation
That occupy the cosmic all
Appear as power vibrations
In a continuum that falls
Within the cosmos in a scale
And as a spectrum band entails
Electromagnetic powers
From which seven powers flower
Through which the waves of light abound
And vibrations Flow as sound
But we have only been told lies
Only what cannot be denied
And we have only been apprised
Of falsehoods that have been devised
To mislead us – we are advised
To be not about vibration
Or the powerful relation
That is a manifestation
Of the relationship within
Us all - that has forever been

SECTION I – PART I

9: VIBRATION

SPIRIT POWER

RAYS OF ALL

ULTRAVIOLET – >

Vibrations ultraviolet
The gamma and the infrared
Radio and microwaves set
Civilization way ahead
As X-rays take us beyond sight
Colors take us within white light
As the red and blue and the yellow
Called the primaries fall below
And within the chromatic scale
The eyes are dazzled with detail
But none will tell us how to use
The other powers or to defuse
The ignorance that has abused
Us all and that has us confused
About who we are as we lose
The vision of our relation
As a spiritual nation
A Spirit civilization
Meant to forever always be
Immortal vibrationally

SECTION I – PART I

10: THROB

VIBRATING – >

THUMPING BEAT

THROBS

Spirit is a vibrating throb
It is a pounding and thumping
Of the within or inside job
Like a continous bumping
That one may hear as vibrating
Powerfully and relating
To an inner motivation
Beginning origination
To the living and to the start
Of the beat of a throbbing heart
But we are not truly informed
Vibrations throb as life conjoins
When all relationships are formed
When everyone alive are born
Spirit throbbing vibrations storm
With the powers of life inside
And within the living abide
Inside with life living alive
And made so by the inside job
Of your spirit's vibrating throb

SECTION I – PART I

10: THROB

VIBRATING

THUMPING BEAT – >

THROBS

The throbbing is a thumping beat
Pounding spirituality
Powerfully throbbing completes
Rhythmatical reality
The music of the spheres vibrate
The thumping throb that procreates
Vibrationally rhythms
In this cosmic organism
This throbbing is a beat alive
Inside with the motive to thrive
But then there are the so called wise
Individuals who have divised
Or who have otherwise contrived
To misdirect us with the lies
Behind which now the real truth hides
The truth that this throbbing delight
Is not just a bump in the night
Or always a reason for fright
That the throb of this vibration
Involves divine connotations

SECTION I – PART I

10: THROB

VIBRATING

THUMPING BEAT

THROBS – >

Power throbs vibrationally
Spirit is a throbbing divine
Ever always throbbingly
Movement within both space and time
The motive and beat of the blood
The throbbing within as a thud
Throbbing within is enchanting
Throbbing is also entrancing
Throbbing can be both disarming
As well as throb can be charming
But throb signs a power that tells
Of Spirit within which we dwell
As power – from which we compel
The powers to move and impel
Ourselves to be and to excel
Given any situation
Given any awful station
Even given bad relations
We may throb power in spirit
Throb with power and endear it

SECTION I – PART I

11: PULSATION

SPIRIT PULSATION – >

PLUS PROCESS

DIVINE

The Spirit is a pulsation
A definite sign of living
Pulsation is the vibration
Of the Spirit of life giving
The living – the motion that lives
Alive by the one that abides –
Pulsation is process and sheer
Rhythm as music of the spheres
The "I AM" power vibration
In the action of pulsation
But we are not taught how to use
The pulse – instead we are confused
And are told only the half truths
We are generally refused
The facts and furthermore abused
In any way to make us regret
Or otherwise make us forget
How to apply the pulse or let
The divine process that it hides
From us be revealed undisguised

SECTION I – PART I

11: PULSATION

SPIRIT PULSATION

PLUS PROCESS – >

DIVINE

The pulse process is in the flow
Processing a motion alive
Within the life – the pulse will go
On as the Spirit will decide
Upon how the pulse of delight
Must be the pulsation of life
The pulsing rhythm is the beat
Of power that only repeats
That "'I AM' all that" vibration
Combination of pulsation
But since the time that we were born
The combinations that conjoin
Pulsations or acts to adorn
Life have been carefully recoined
Or hidden – now today we mourn
The loss of the intimacy
We had with ourselves knowlingly
When we completely trusted the
The information that pulsation
Gave us about each sensation

SECTION I – PART I

11: PULSATION

SPIRIT PULSATION

PLUS PROCESS

DIVINE – >

Pulsation is Spirit divine
Electromagnetically
The rhythm within space of time
It signs "I AM" divinity
Defines the movement called living
It is that "I AM" that giving
As the Spirit which pulsation
Is both sign and realization
Pulsing life living as the sign
In this realness moving as time
But this is not all - there is more
About this Spirit to adore
Much more exists here to explore
Or intimately look out for
When using the pulsation and or
Living rhythmatic vibrations
Communicating sensations
That informs of situations
We may never know all about
As long as we are kept in doubt

SECTION I – PART I

12: UNDULATION

                                              THE VIBRATION – >

UNDULATES

ITS OWN UNITY

The undulation vibration
Is the Spirit of the power
Divinity undulations
And vibrations that tower
More powerfully than static
Vibrate electromagnetic
Undulations of power waves
Expressing the entire phase
Of spectral vibrations that lie
As powers and that occupy
All nature – but intimately
We all who know can but barely
Distinguish the it from the me
From the "I AM" powerfully
Thus because this is actively
A point on which we are confused
Misinformers readily use
This mass confusion to infuse
Misinformation and devise
To misdirect us all with lies

SECTION I – PART I

12: UNDULATION

THE VIBRATION

UNDULATES – >

ITS OWN UNITY

The cosmic Spirit undulates
Divinity personified
It spiritually vibrates
So its presence be realized
And understood powerfully
Electro-magnetically
As every undulation
Is a powerful vibration
Spirits undulate in power
Just like blossoms into flowers
But we're not taught to recognize
Nor to consciously realize
When attempts are made to apprise
Us of the truth or otherwise
Inform us of facts or revise
The false facts or the false program
That has been used on us in scams
To make us disbelieve "'I AM'
The spirit herein remaking
My self as 'I AM' creating"

12: UNDULATION

THE VIBRATION

UNDULATES

ITS OWN UNITY – >

A part of its own trinity
Undulation is vibration
And with throbbing the unity
Existing in these relations
Between pulsation and the throb
Completes the divine inside job
Electromagnetically
Spiritual divinity
Uses powerful vibrations
Throbbing pulse and undulations
But no one is supposed to know
Nor is anyone supposed to show
The ignorant that power flows
As the basis of life below
And above all as it follows
The life of each and all of us
As a motive both true and just
And only used when we can trust
That everyone will vibrate
With power when we undulate

SECTION I – PART II

13: ENERGY

SPIRITUALITY – >

OF MATTER

ENERGETIC

Energy spiritually
As vim vigor and liveliness
In power is vitality
Expressing divine consciousness
In the trinity energy
Contributes to the synergy
Between vibrations and force
From which there can be no divorce
The trinities of energies
In Spirit shall ever be
But trinities inside power
And in the "I AM ALL" flowers
As a tower of the power
– As an "I AM" power shower –
Of energies within power
But by deception and by scam
We are intimately programmed
To deny being the "I AM"
Power of the divinity
And Spirit of all energy

SECTION I – PART II

13: ENERGY

SPIRITUALITY

OF MATTER – >

ENERGETIC

All of matter is energy
As vibration at the highest
Form of matter – a trinity
Of activity and no less
An electromagnetical
Arraying of the powerful
A spectrum of the energies
Of life for a free life of ease
As these energies can provide
More than just living to survive
But socially today's design
By the power mongers define
Life and suggest that all resign
And do not ever be inclined
To spiritually refine
The spiritual expression
And the powerful direction
Of energetic vibrations
That all might live a life of ease
With spiritual energies

13: ENERGY

SPIRITUALITY

OF MATTER

ENERGETIC – >

Spirit energetically
Appears as a divinity
Electromagnetically
Spirit expresses trinity
And activity in being
Thus the power in believing
Operates to bring about ends
Or goals that the Spirit intends
For motion is the energy
Of "I AM" creating "to be"
But since we have been made to stay
As far as we can be away
From truth about ourselves today
We are now forced and made to pay
For energy every day
And also made or forced to learn
That living this life must be earned
That we must only be concerned
With payment and never with free
Energy spiritually

SECTION I – PART II

14: VIGOR

IN SPIRIT – >

POWERFUL

VIGOR OF LIFE

Vigor in Spirit is a kind
Of motive for intensity
Defying the rhythm of time
When "I AM" all activity
Within its trinity this vigor
With lively vim is a trigger
Of that powerful energy
That everyone sees as me
In Spirit "I AM" vigorous
As in Spirit are all of us
But we are actively depressed
And kept away from happiness
And hale and from the hardiness
And also kept full of distress
So we know not vigorousness
Or the intense vivacity
Found within the activity
Of vigor and vitality
Vigor is raw dynamism
Spirit as an organism

SECTION I – PART II

14: VIGOR

IN SPIRIT

POWERFUL – >

VIGOR OF LIFE

Vigorously powerful rules
The action of the energy
Not taught about within the schools
Teaching of the power to be
Yet as Spirit vigor persist
As divine power to exist
The energy of life giving
Drive and gusto in the living
Vigor is enthusiasm
Intimately in orgasms
But we are not supposed to say
That vigorousness is that way
That with it there is no delay
That instantly it will allay
All of your wishes and you pay
No one for your vigor or verve
For vitality or the nerve
To have what you wish and not swerve
To vigorously enjoy it
As the vigor of your Spirit

SECTION I – PART II

14: VIGOR

IN SPIRIT

POWERFUL

VIGOR OF LIFE – >

Spirit is the vigor of life
The hardiness to sustain
The verve needed to avoid strife
Enthusiasm to maintain
The active course of the spirit
In operations when it hits
Dynamically chosen goals
Vigorously charged to the soul
As actions designed to retain
What vigor in Spirit attains
But power mad societies
Have decided vigorously
That vigor is not supposed to be
Known by the masses powerfully
Nor used by the masses to be free
Of unrealities that bind
The Spirit of vigor with time
And within sluggishness confine
Vigor to an ignorantly
Beheld idea impotently

SECTION I – PART II

15: VIM

OVER THE TOP – >

AS VIM

RELISH WITH APPETITE

Vim is vigor over the top
It is Spirit over the rim
It is the most powerful hop
Expressing Spirit ... it is vim
Spiritual vitality
Dynamic in reality
Infatuation at its best
In life a joy in consciousness
Divinely a Spirit that crams
Its self best into the "I AM"
But vim's vigor is exploited
Its birth as sacred Aborted
As the "money mad" resorted
To the most insanely sordid
Actions that could be imparted
To the actions that vim infuse
And activities that vigor used
To signal Spirit and not lose
The Spirit of integrity
Performing spiritually

SECTION I – PART II

15: VIM

OVER THE TOP

VIM EXPRESSES – >

RELISH WITH APPETITE

Vim expresses divinity
Of Spirit – we all stand witness
To that entity of energy
Moving the consciousness with bliss
For vim is delight in passion
Enthusiasm in fashion
Vim is used to socially move
The masses and not to abuse
Ignorance or to covertly rob
Them using vim to do the job
But we are uneducated
About how vim is related
Or otherwise situated
In life ... that vim co-created
Pleasure and invigorated
Spiritual realism
With lively eroticism
And a raw animalism
By being true expressively
And zestful spiritually

SECTION I – PART II

15: VIM

OVER THE TOP

AS VIM

RELISH WITH APPETITE – >

Vim is relish with appetite
Infatuation with ardor
Vim is an excited craze bright
With an obsessive gusto for
The keenness and fervor of dash
May be inclined toward the rash
Spirit as a raw energy
Active in personality
As individuality
Vim is joyful reality
But we're not suppose to impart
Or to otherwise have a part
To play consciously at the heart
Of the reality that starts
As the vim about life that marks
The presence of divinity
About every entity
In life – for in reality
All may fill the cup to the brim
With the Spirit of life called vim

SECTION I – PART II

16: LIVELINESS

DIVINE CONSCIOUSNESS – >

DISGUISES SPIRIT

MOST LIVELY

The life of divine consciousness
As Spirit and divinity
Expresses "I AM" liveliness
As dazzling vitality
Continuously shimmering
Energetic and glimmering
The life around the "get-up-and-go"
The glint around the inside glow
Liveliness is vivacity
Twinkling as reality
But we were not suppose to display
Liveliness and sparkle this way
Unless lively was done for pay
We were supposed to keep this ray
Living within ourselves away
From others and not let the glow
Or that living "get-up-and-go"
(Without getting paid for it) flow
We are taught to sell the spirit
Sell the Spirit for a profit

SECTION I – PART II

16: LIVELINESS

DIVINE CONSCIOUSNESS

DISGUISES SPIRIT – >

MOST LIVELY

Liveliness disguises Spirit
That around which Spirit abides
We all have learned to endear it
As the lively of the alive
As the vibration of shimmer
As the elation in glimmer
As the sparkle in the flicker
As the glint flashing in glitter
As the obsession known in rage
As infatuation engaged
But Spirit can be really known
In power as power and shown
By the power as the alone
That is vibrating through its own
Energy as ether or stone
But the power hungry devised
To exploit the spirit's disguise
By maintaining the social lies
About your true relatedness
As the life living liveliness

SECTION I – PART II

16: LIVELINESS

DIVINE CONSCIOUSNESS

DISGUISES SPIRIT

MOST LIVELY – >

The cosmic all is most lively
And the most active expression
Of the Spirit – advisedly
A universal perfection
Universally liveliness
Or divinity will express
The divine manifestation
Without any complication
Of energies or of powers
Or the liveliness that flowers
But – "I AM" actuality
Perfectly through vitality
The "I AM" all reality
About all as vivacity
The "I AM I" that all calls me
That only those upon some throne
Will claim – they say that they alone
Can claim that they alone can own
By honor or acclaim the right
To liveliness – many calls might

SECTION I – PART III

17: FORCE

COMPLETES THE TRINITY – >

ENECTROMAGNETICALLY

OF STRENGTH

The force completes the trinity
As the Spirit of the power
That expresses divinity
With energy vibes that empower
That becoming "I AM" to be
Electromagnetically
Force is both influence and strength
Combined with might and really sent
To be and not ever quit it
As force of the sacred Spirit
But we are not all made aware
Of how intimately the forces fare
About us – we're taught to beware
Of the forces and never dare
Probe or access the sacred lair
Where around the forces abide
About powerfully alive
The forces that forever strive
With vibrations and energy
To only be powerfully

SECTION I – PART III

17: FORCE

COMPLETES THE TRINITY

ENECTROMAGNETICALLY – >

OF STRENGTH

Electromagnetically
Forces appear as spectral waves
As a spirituality
Universally the forces play
Throughout the being of all things
The force of sacred living brings
Ultraviolet and X-rays
Radio and the microwave
With the gamma rays and white light
Include seven names that they cite
But these aren't all of the forces
Known to be currently coursing
Through us – yet they are divorcing
Us from these and other forces
As yet unknown to be coursing
And access to them are denied
Until a payment is applied
Or until all are otherwise
Made to serve those who secretly
Control the forces completely

17: FORCE

COMPLETES THE TRINITY

ENECTROMAGNETICALLY

OF STRENGTH – >

Force is the influence of strength
And is also the strength of might
Force is the power that is meant
To abide the Spirit of right
The forces of divinity
Bring powers of the trinity
To bear upon the consciousness
That "I AM" all - the forces impress
All with an awareness to be
What "I AM" wanting forcefully
But forces driven with delight
Blazing passion and appetite
With gusto and glint glowing bright
With the "get-up-and-go" of flight
Have been afflicted with the blight
And might of a social taboo
To prevent me and to stop you
From knowing the forcefully true
And correct nature about life
Within and about without strife

SECTION I – PART III

18: INFLUENCE

AS FORCE – >

IN STRESS

IS DIVINITY

Influence as force can vary
As a spiritual power
Influence will sway and carry
Clout and influence can flower
With authority and likewise
Spirit as influence can rise
Within force and manipulate
All of the forces with the weight
Of the influence of Spirit
Influencing the lives near it
But the power brokers must sell
Influence – they would never tell
Nor disclose how they can compel
And pressure others or expel
Or dethrone rulers – no, they dwell
In secrecy and seclusion
Where they maintain the illusion
Of a dumb-numbing confusion
That Influence is not an act
Expressing the Spirit in fact

18: INFLUENCE

AS FORCE

IN STRESS –>

IS DIVINITY

Spirit is influence in stress
With affect an inspiration
Influence sways the consciousness
As a basic motivation
Influence shapes and bears upon
The last word before clout has gone
Persuading and winning over
All – above which control hovers –
Influence is divinity
Raw and uncut authority
But the masses must not possess
Influence or have the access
To an effective force unless
They pay or can clearly impress
With influence or with finesse
Those who would grant or would permit
The common folk of life to sit
Among and with them in spirit
And let the commoners say so
Induce and Influence the flow

SECTION I – PART III

18: INFLUENCE

AS FORCE

IN STRESS

IS DIVINITY – >

Influence is divinity
Very forceful as a power
With strength and might a trinity
Of power that truly towers
As a force mysteriously
Unsubtle imperiously
Influence controls and commands
Influence is pressured demand
The way to both manipulate
And to covertly stipulate
But very few can acquire
The force needed or aspire
To a powerfully higher
Source without being a buyer
Of influence – a desire
In Spirit – powerfully meant
Influences all with a hint
That persuades and compels intent
Induces clout and changes course
And influences using force

SECTION I – PART III

19: STRENGTH

POTENCY – >

A MUSCLE RIGHTLY

POWER STRONG

Potency is measurable
As power or force of the strength
Of Spirit and the durable
Quality of the Spirit meant
Potently when strength impresses
The power that Spirit stresses
Strength means with potency strongly
The muscle rightly or wrongly
The degree expressing spirit
For one to endear or fear it
But we are told that a man's strength
Expressions are unreal and meant
To only be an apparent
Showy display without intent
These lies were designed to imprint
An incorrect understanding
Upon our minds and commanding
A following by demanding
That a mans strength and his appeal
Appears more apparent than real

SECTION I – PART III

19: STRENGTH

POTENCY

A MUSCLE RIGHTLY – >

POWER STRONG

Strength works like a muscle – rightly
Or wrongly – expressing spirit
Forcefully – strength is a tightly
Held force for those that will fear it
The raw muscle of the power
Of the Spirit – and it flowers
In all the manifestations
Of energy-force vibrations
Strength is "I AM" powerfully
As a living divinity
But socially we all are taught
To challenge strength – that strength is naught
But a vagrant and abstract thought
That strength needs never to be brought
Up seriously or be sought
Out unless done so in the name
Of play and should be made a game
Or an objective end for fame
And not ever should it be meant
To be known in Spirit as strength

SECTION I – PART III

19: STRENGTH

POTENCY

A MUSCLE RIGHTLY

POWER STRONG – >

Strength is known as the power strong
When strong is the strength to be tough
Strength knows neither right nor the wrong
When right or the wrong can mean rough
Strength is virtue as the essence
Of power that the Spirit sent
Within the manifestation
Of any force filled relation
Strength is the way to really know
If the Spirit really can flow
But deceivers definitely
Do not want the masses to see
That life can be meaningfully
Powerful spiritually
And strong with true strength forcefully
No, they would have the masses weak
Making sure that people will seek
To pay for their help and stay meek
And never come to realize
What the deceivers have devised

SECTION I – PART III

20: MIGHT

MIGHT IS DIVINE – >

FORCE

RIGHTEOUSLY

Might is divine force like a voice
Of influence and of the strength
Truly representing the choice
That the Spirit made when it meant
All to know once and all for true
That might meant here is sent from you
The might completes the trinity
Of forces of divinity
Might is that motive that selects
Strong muscle potent in effect
But misleaders about the spirit
Would not have us all endear it
Would stop us from coming near it
Would have us all only fear it
And not know the self as spirit
They would keep the information
About the forceful relation
We have – in Spirit – away from
Us and keep the effects of might
Spiritually out-of-sight

SECTION I – PART III

20: MIGHT

MIGHT IS DIVINE

FORCE – >

RIGHTEOUSLY

Powerful is the force of might
As divine Spirit - it towers
Over all as the "I AM" right
When seen as a forceful power
Might is always truly about
Effective power without doubt
And affective ultimately
To bring about reality
To actually be by might
Needs little knowledge or insight
But mighty spirits are called brutes
By those that would really refute
That might is the right or dispute
The Spirit of might and dilute
Or vanquish might unless it suits
The motives of those that have tried
To monopolize might with lies
Or that have otherwise devised
To keep exclusive the insight
Concerning the knowledge of might

SECTION I – PART III

20: MIGHT

MIGHT IS DIVINE

FORCE

RIGHTEOUSLY – >

Spirit is righteously might
It ends mortality and weak
Groveling with forceful insight
It is what divinity seeks
When the "I AM' divinity
Conveys spirituality
It is the powerful recall
Of the All-Mighty cosmic all
Motivation of the spirit
All may endear and not fear it
But functions of the status quo
Stipulates that no one must grow
To come to understand or know
The way out of the social flow
And with the might of Spirit go
Blaze new avenues of delight
Approaching challenges to fight
Anew and righteously with might
Regain conscious reality
And the right to BE mightily

"Seek not to follow in the footsteps of the wise.

Seek what they sought."
(Quoted by Dr. Sandy Jacobs of The Circle's Edge Spiritual Center)

THE SPIRIT
IS
THE COSMIC ALL - POWER

ABOUT THE AUTHOR

Malcolm L. Landry has been a "relatively unknown" poetic writer for 50 years. Since the turn of the millennium, Mr. Landry's work has been printed on poetry.com and in two books published by the International Society Of Poets, which society also awarded him certificates of recognition. The Author may be contacted via e-mail at cap1341@yahoo.com or by writing to: Malcolm L. Landry, 352 Lake Street #214, Reno, NV 89501 Please include your telephone number in all correspondences.

Printed in the United States
by Baker & Taylor Publisher Services

Printed in the United States
by Baker & Taylor Publisher Services